Pioneering Women

THE COLLEGE FOR WOMEN
(GIRTON COLLEGE, CAMBRIDGE)
OPENED AND REMAINED HERE
16th. OCTOBER 1869 - JUNE 1873

Miss Townshend. Miss Woodhead. Miss Gibson.
Miss Cook. Miss Lumsden.

Pioneering Women

The origins of
Girton College in Hitchin

Val Campion

A Hitchin Historical Society Publication

For my granddaughters
Charlotte, Flora and Isabel
May they benefit fully from the
endeavours of these pioneering women

By the same author: *Joseph Ransom's Naturalist's Notebook*

Copyright © Val Campion & Hitchin Historical Society

ISBN 978-0-9552411-3-0

Design by Barrie Dack and Associates, Tel: 01462 834640.
Printed by The Lion Press, Sandy, Bedfordshire

Cover photograph:	The students at the College, Benslow House, Hitchin 1871
Inside front cover:	OS 25" map of Hitchin dated 1898, showing the location of Benslow House
Half title page:	Plaque commemorating the College, outside Benslow House in 2008
Frontispiece:	Students in the garden, 1870
Inside back cover:	"OS 25" map of Hitchin, 1881

Contents

Acknowledgements

I am deeply indebted to the following, without whom this book would not have come to fruition:

Kate Perry, Girton College's archivist, for making archive material available to me, and for all the assistance she has given me.

Lorraine Screene, the Westfield College Archivist at Queen Mary College, London, for material relating to Constance Maynard.

My husband, Phil Rowe, for his invaluable technical assistance, support and encouragement and for the photographs on the half-title page and page 60.

The Hitchin Historical Society publications team, Scilla Douglas and Pauline Humphries, without whom this book would not have been possible.

David Hodges, Derek Wheeler and Keith Fitzpatrick-Matthews of the North Herts Museum Service, for supply of photographs and other source material.

Steve Pearce, for his wide knowledge of all railway matters, to Carola Scupham and Bridget Howlett of Hitchin Historical Society for their invaluable assistance, and to Charles Rowe, Derek Wheeler and Zena Grant for their proof-reading skills.

The Mistress and Fellows of Girton College, Cambridge for photographs on pages i, viii, 8, 18, 36, 53 including cameos within chapters 3 and 5.

Hitchin Museum for photographs onthe cover, page 58 including cameos within chapters 3 and 5.

Barrie Dack for his skill in layout and production.

Val Campion
October 2008

Foreword

Many of those who visit Girton College, Cambridge today, and stand in admiration in front of the magnificent red-brick Waterhouse buildings set in extensive grounds, have little appreciation of the College's beginnings in a Victorian villa in Hitchin, Hertfordshire.

Val Campion's study of the origins of 'The College for Women' at Benslow House will do much to redress this situation. Of course the established College histories, and more general works on women's education, make mention of the four academic years that the College was established at Hitchin, but this is the first time that there has been an exclusive study of this period.

As a resident of Hitchin, living close to Benslow House, and member of Hitchin Historical Society, Val Campion is ideally placed to write this history. She has used material in Girton archive, as well as local sources, to create profiles of the first women to receive exactly the same kind of University education as that open to their male contemporaries, and to illustrate their lives at College, and beyond.

Most importantly, given that Hitchin was chosen for its convenient position on the railway line between London and Cambridge, she has included information about the lecturers who came to instruct these pioneering women.

The College for Women at Benslow House may have been described by a passing clergyman as 'that infidel place' but for the students who studied there it offered 'the delights of privacy, the chance of knowledge for its own sake ... a glorious prospect'.

Kate Perry
Archivist
Girton College, Cambridge
October 2008

Benslow House, Hitchin in 1869 – the year the College opened

The Girton Pioneers

Tune: *The British Grenadiers*

Some talk of Senior Wranglers,
And some of Double Firsts,
And truly of their species
These are not the worst;
But of all the Cambridge heroes
There's none that can compare
With Woodhead, Cook and Lumsden,
The Girton Pioneers.

Whenever we go forward
A hard exam to try,
Their memory goes before us
To raise our courage high.
They made old Cambridge wonder;
Then let us give three cheers
For Woodhead, Cook and Lumsden,
The Girton Pioneers.

And when the goal is won, girls,
And women get degrees,
We'll cry, "Long live the three, girls,
Who showed the way to these!
Who showed the way we follow,
Who knew no doubts or fears,
Our Woodhead, Cook and Lumsden,
The Girton Pioneers!"

Then let us fill a tea-cup
And drink a health to those
Who studied well and played well,
As everybody knows,
May we fulfil the promise,
Of Girton's earliest years,
Of Woodhead, Cook and Lumsden,
The Girton Pioneers!

Introduction

The Seeds of a Dream

There is a story, which may be apocryphal, about an occasion in the Garrett family home in Aldeburgh, Suffolk, in 1860, where Elizabeth Garrett and her friend, Emily Davies, and Elizabeth's younger sister, Millicent, were discussing their futures. Elizabeth was determined to enter the medical profession, then closed to women; Emily's ambition was to make higher education available to women, and that left women's franchise for Millicent to address.

Elizabeth, who became Elizabeth Garrett Anderson, did enter the medical profession, Millicent became Millicent Fawcett and strove to secure the vote for women, and Emily devoted her life to the cause of higher education for women, founding Girton College, Cambridge.

In the mid-nineteenth century it was not considered necessary to educate girls beyond a level needed to run a home efficiently: reading, writing, simple arithmetic, and a few gentle accomplishments, such as needlework, drawing and music, were all that was needed. There were, however, some schools for girls that offered more: North London Collegiate School for Girls, founded in 1850 by

Frances Buss, and Cheltenham Ladies' College, of which Dorothea Beale became head in 1858, were two such establishments. Miss Buss and Miss Beale were to become synonymous with the cause of women's education.

Emily Davies was not fortunate enough to attend either of these schools but her burning ambition was to enable women to benefit from the same kind of higher education that was open to men. In England at that time, that meant Oxford, Cambridge or London Universities or The Victoria University, Manchester. Bedford College for Women had opened at 47 (now 48) Bedford Square as a day college for women as part of London University in 1848, but women were not admitted to either Oxford or Cambridge.

The opposition to this ambition was enormous. It was seriously believed that women's health would suffer from academic study and that they would lose their femininity. Emily Davies was, however, undaunted and set about realising her dream, a dream that was to begin its path to fruition in the little Hertfordshire market town of Hitchin in 1869.

Emily Davies c. 1866

Chapter 1

Emily Davies

Born in 1830, the daughter of a clergyman, Emily Davies experienced a life all too typical of a young woman of her class and situation. Her father, John Davies, seems to have been a frustrated academic. He was ordained into the Church of England and just before Emily was born he applied for the post of professor of moral and political philosophy at London University.

The post, however, could not guarantee a stipend of £300 a year and he withdrew his application. When Emily was born he was headmaster of a small boys' boarding school. During her childhood her father's health, possibly both physical and mental, was not good, and the family moved several times, eventually to Gateshead where he was offered a living.

The rectory was a large rambling house which required a great deal of work, keeping Emily's mother Mary and her sister Jane busy. The Rev. John Davies, however, was much happier in this situation with three churches to oversee with the help of two curates. Unfortunately he did not see the need to educate his daughters.

Sadly, by 1857 three of his five children had died leaving just Emily and her oldest brother, Llewelyn. Llewelyn was a curate in Limehouse and so it fell to Emily to care for her grieving parents. (One of her brothers, Henry, had died in Algiers and Emily had been sent to nurse him.)

Whilst there she met Barbara Bodichon (née Leigh-Smith), a meeting that was to change her life. Barbara Bodichon was an extraordinary woman for her time, with revolutionary views on the status of women and their education and she had a profound effect on Emily.

Once Emily had returned home to Gateshead she tried to continue with her parish duties and to do a little teaching but became frustrated by her own lack of education.

In the spring of 1859 Emily visited Llewelyn in London and met Barbara again, and also Elizabeth Garrett, who became Elizabeth Garrett Anderson, and Bessie Parkes who was an indefatigable campaigner for higher education for women.

In 1866 Bessie Parkes and Barbara Bodichon formed the first ever Women's Suffrage Committee. (Bessie Parkes married Louis Belloc. They had two children, one of whom was the poet, Hilaire Belloc.)

The Bodichon home at 19 Langham Place became the headquarters of the newly formed Society for the Employment of Women. Gradually Emily's dream of a college for women was beginning to take shape but she was still tied to her parents and the rectory in Gateshead.

This was all to change when her father died unexpectedly in 1860. Within six months her mother had moved to London and Emily was back in the centre of the Langham Place set and its influences. Emily began to campaign for the right of women to enter university and study for a degree.

Apart from enormous opposition to the idea there was also the problem of where the students were to come from. Miss Beale was working hard to improve girls' education at Cheltenham Ladies' College and Miss Buss was doing the same at North London Collegiate School for Girls, but very few other establishments offered anything like a satisfactory education for girls.

In 1858 Local Examinations had been introduced to standardise education in the many independent schools, including those for girls, and HM Inspectors were already overseeing the standards in the National Schools, which were for both girls and boys. Things were beginning to improve.

Over the next few years Emily worked to improve further the standard of education for girls but her dream was to found a college where they could study at the same level as the men in the universities of Oxford, Cambridge and London. From early in 1865 Emily was writing frequently to her friend Anna Richardson and to Barbara Bodichon about the plans for the college.

Finally, in 1867, she set up a committee for just this purpose. Barbara Bodichon was the first to donate £1,000 followed by many other notable men and women, among them George Eliot who, as 'The Author of Romola,' donated £50.

Next was the problem of a site for the college. Generally speaking, Cambridge was more sympathetic to the idea than Oxford but even Cambridge would not countenance a college for women being established actually in Cambridge and so a site with proximity to Cambridge was sought.

Anna Richardson was a Quaker and had connections with Quakers in Hitchin, among them James Hack Tuke and Frederick Seebohm, the bankers, who also knew Alfred Ransom, another prominent member of the Religious Society of Friends in Hitchin. Alfred's father, John Ransom, had died two years before and left his home, Benslow House, to his son, who had let it on a lease.

The lease had expired and, through Frederick Seebohm and Anna Richardson, Emily came to hear of it and visited the house to see if it would be suitable. One great advantage was that it was a short walk from the railway station on the line between London and Cambridge, which would enable visiting lecturers to come from either university. It was agreed that Benslow House would be the location for the College and a lease was taken for three years.

In the meantime Emily had to recruit the students. Advertisements were placed in various periodicals such as the article Emily's brother, Llewelyn, placed in Macmillan's Magazine, headed 'A New College for Women'. He stated that:

> *Its general aim is to offer young women of the same class the aids which these Colleges have provided for young men… The proposed College will be a new thing… it will provide separate rooms and a liberal system of discipline, it will seek to obtain the services of the most competent teachers; and it will endeavour to secure an examination of a fixed University standard, to be passed at the end of the course. It is suggested that the College should be placed at some point most easily accessible from London and Cambridge. Residence will not take up more than half a year.*

Once Hitchin had been decided upon, an article appeared in the local paper on June 27th 1868, headed, 'A Ladies College in Hitchin'. This reflected a certain amount of pride in the venture, ending with the paragraph:

We should become renowned not only for our barley, and plait, and lavender, but for the establishment of the first women's College in England.

Queen Elizabeth I had professed a preference for Hitchin ale; straw plaiting for hats was an important part of the domestic economy and lavender was grown in the fields around Hitchin for the manufacture of lavender water and other lavender-based products.

Articles and advertisements like this produced enquiries from women all over the country, but now that the dream was becoming a reality opposition to it was growing.

Even the *Manchester Guardian* pronounced, 'a girl's proper university is in her own home in the bosom of her family.' Undaunted, Emily replied, 'why should intellectual excellence be incompatible with domestic virtues...?'

It was, however, imperative that the girls should be of a high enough academic standard and reluctantly Emily agreed to an entrance examination. Men entering Oxford and Cambridge were not required to take an entrance examination and Emily wanted equality for women from the start, but she was acutely aware of the deficiencies of girls' education and wanted to be sure they would be able to cope with the curriculum of the College.

July 3rd 1869 was the date of the first entrance examination and eighteen young women attended. The results were mixed but ten candidates passed the examination and all were eager to try for the honours degree.

In the event only five women took up their places in the first intake of students, paying fees of £105 a year, arriving at Benslow House on 16th October 1869. In the following week Emily wrote to Barbara Bodichon: the students 'work together beautifully... We are most fortunate in the lecturers, especially Mr Clark, the Classical teacher, & Mr Hort. It is delightful to hear a language taught as Mr Clark teaches Latin. It is so thoroughly intelligent and interesting' and reported to her that Adelaide Manning 'ejaculates, "it is so pleasant to be at the College"...' Adelaide was the stepdaughter of Charlotte Manning, the Mistress of the College. Although she had taken the entrance exam and took up her place at the college, Adelaide had decided not to take any further examinations.

Within a week or so of the opening of the College Emily Davies asked Barbara when she would be visiting, warning her that 'We have not got salt spoons yet & are using sticks for pokers, but otherwise we are civilised.'

And so, after so many years of hard work and determination, with so many obstacles to overcome, Emily Davies had at last achieved her dream and the College was open, even if it was without salt spoons.

Chapter 2

The Students

T he first students arrived at Benslow House, Hitchin, on 16th October 1869. They were Emily Gibson, Anna Lloyd, Louisa Lumsden, Isabella Townshend and Sarah Woodhead. Rachel Cook had also been accepted but was prevented by ill health from joining the others until after Christmas.

Emily Gibson (1849-1934) was the first applicant to the College. She was in Heidelberg during the early part of 1868 and heard of the College from a Russian lady who had seen the article by Emily Davies' brother, Llewelyn, in *Macmillan's Magazine*. She had received some education as a child at a school in Clapham but this came to an end before she was sixteen because of money problems in the family. In the *Girton Review* of 1925 she states that she 'was

Standing: Sarah Woodhead, Anna Lloyd, Louisa Lumsden
Seated: Emily Gibson and Isabella Townshend
The 'College Five' at Benslow House, Autumn 1869

longing for an opportunity for study'. She was aware that her education was somewhat lacking and wrote to Emily Davies asking what she should do. Miss Davies advised her to study Latin and mathematics, which she did, though with a shortage of both money and tutors this was not easy. However, when Emily took the entrance exam in June 1869 she was placed 5th.

Louisa Innes Lumsden (1840-1935)  was 28 when she arrived at Benslow. She grew up in Aberdeen and was the seventh and youngest child of Clements Lumsden and his wife, Jane. She was taught to read before the age of six by her nurse and then shared a governess with her sisters for a short while. After the death of her father the family moved to Cheltenham where Louisa attended school for the first time, before going to boarding school in Belgium.

On her return to England she attended a finishing school in London which she found dull after the happy years she had spent in Belgium. On returning to Scotland in 1857 she continued to educate herself and when she heard of a course of lectures for women given by professors at Edinburgh University she enrolled at once. Towards the end of the 1860s Louisa heard Emily Davies was about to open a college for women and, with the support of her mother, though against the wishes of other members of the family, she applied, took the entrance exam and was accepted.

Anna Lloyd (b.1837) was, like Sarah Woodhead, born into a Quaker family. Her father, Samuel Lloyd, was a mine owner. The Religious Society of Friends has always been assiduous at providing education for their children and there were good schools for girls as well as boys. Anna Lloyd, however, was educated at home and in Switzerland, Italy and Paris. In later life she wrote a memoir in which she describes the years before and her time at the College. She spent 1867 to 1869 travelling in Europe, spending the spring of 1869 in Paris with her cousins Rachel and Dora Albright.

In June 1869, having returned home, she wrote to a friend, Mary E. Waterhouse, using the Quaker form of address, 'Thou ask me for my plans. I wonder what thou wilt say to them when thou hears them. I am frightened of myself for since I came to London I have seen Miss Davies and she has brought back again college to my mind and impresses upon me that it is my duty to enter in October.'

By July 1869 she was 'working hard for the examination five hours a day and more if I can get it. I have eight subjects to get up and my coachman reckoned I have only sixty hours for each before the end of September.'

On 20th September she wrote, 'I am in great state for this day fortnight I go to London for the exam and feel quite blank of knowledge... Arithmetic is hopeless.' In the event she did not register as a student but attended the College as an observer for about a year.

She did not return to the College after the Christmas vacation in January 1871 because her siblings were putting pressure on her, claiming she was neglecting her duties as a daughter.

Isabella Frances Vere Townshend, (1847-1882) was the daughter of an English family living in Ireland. Little is known of her life before going to the College and, though she won a scholarship for her excellence in essay writing, she did not stay until the end of the course. She later lived in Rome and was an artist, dying of typhoid in Capri in 1882.

Sarah Woodhead (1851-1875) was, at 18, the youngest of the first students at the College. Born into a Quaker family in Manchester she was educated at the Quaker schools at Ackworth and York. She won an entrance scholarship for excellence in mathematics and Class I in both parts of the Previous Exam in 1870. She was the first woman to take the Mathematics Tripos and passed 'Senior Optima'.

Rachel Susan Cook, (1848-1905) was the daughter of the Rev. John Cook, a professor at St Andrews University, and his wife, Rachel Susan Farquhar. She was educated at home and at the age of 20 applied to the College. She was accepted and, though due to start with the other

students in October 1869, she was prevented by ill health and joined the College in January 1870.

She was the first woman to attempt the Classical Tripos at Cambridge, gaining a second class in 1873.

1870

Isabella Hariette Gamble *right* (b.1851), **G. M. Slade**, (b.1842) and **Ellen Elizabeth Tidman,** attended the College from October 1870 but little is known about them, and they all left after a short time.

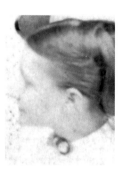

1871

Mary Kingsland (1854-1937) was born in Devizes in Wiltshire, the daughter of William and Caroline Kingsland. Her father was a congregational minister, and in 1862 he became the minister at College Chapel, Bradford in Yorkshire. Mary was educated at home with her brothers until she went to the local Miss Scott's school when she was thirteen. In 1871 she won an exhibition to the College for Women in Hitchin. She was the first woman to take Cambridge's Natural Science Tripos, gaining second-class honours.

Elizabeth Welsh, (1843-1921) was born on 3rd March 1843 in County Down, Ireland. She was educated at home and at private schools in Ireland. The clergyman of her local church taught her Greek and Latin. She may have heard about the College from Isabella Townshend, who also came from Ireland and joined the College in its first year in 1869.

Agnes Amy Bulley, (1852-1939) known as Amy, was born at Liscard, New Brighton, Cheshire in 1852. Her father was a cotton broker and he and his wife, Mary Rachel Bulley, held progressive views on women's education. They were influenced by Anne Jemima Clough, a family friend who later became the first warden of Newnham College, Cambridge. Amy studied at Laleham School, Clapham before becoming a student at the College. She was one of the first two women (the other was Mary Paley, a Newnham student) to sit for the Moral Science Tripos in 1874, being placed in the second class.

Jane Frances Dove (1847-1942), known as Frances, was the daughter of the Rev. John Thomas Dove, a clergyman in the Church of England, and his wife Jane Ding. She and her two brothers were first taught by their father at home in London.

At this time the Rev. Dove was curate to the Rev. Llewelyn Davies, rector of Christ Church, Marylebone, who was the brother of Emily Davies.

After her father had been moved to the parish of Cowbit in Lincolnshire, Frances asked to go to boarding school, but she later described it as being 'everything a school should not be'. On returning home she was kept busy with the younger children and parish duties. She was 24 before she applied to the College and, though she prepared for the entrance exam without the benefit of tuition, she was successful, her performance in the arithmetic exam being outstanding.

Rose Aitken (1848-1923) won a scholarship to the College and took the Classical Tripos in 1875.

Mary Hoskins (b.1850) left Girton College in 1874, having taken only the Previous exam.

1872

Constance Mary Maynard, (1849-
1935) was born on 19th February 1849
at Highbury, Middlesex. She grew up in
Hawkhurst in Kent and was educated at
home and at Belstead School in Suffolk,
though she was there for only one year.
She kept several diaries simultaneously
for different purposes. In what she
called her 'Green Books' she kept a
record of the sermons she heard, where

they had been delivered and by whom. On weekdays she
would take a text and study it, writing her thoughts in the
Green Book. Alongside this she kept a personal journal
in which she recorded the day-to-day events of her life
and sometimes copied into it letters she received. In the
winter of 1871/72 she spent several weeks with relations
in St Andrews in Scotland and, encouraged by her cousin
Lewis, took advantage of the open lectures at St Andrews
University. These were held in the afternoons and covered
several different subjects.

Dr Bell lectured on the circulation of the blood in the
heart and lungs. She was so enthused by this that she
acquired an ox heart and, together with a friend, Isabella
Cook, dissected it. She records that it was quite successful,
'but [we] got a little lost in its arteries, though we saw the
valves beautifully.'

Isabella Cook was a relation of Rachel Cook, who was
already at the College, and Constance corresponded with
her and with Cousin Lewis about the College. In May
Rachel sent Constance 'a whole bundle of exam papers,

which appear formidable.' However she was not daunted and spent hours each day studying, assisted by her brother George.

By 10th May 1872 she had got the 'willing consent of both Father and Mother to my going for one year to the College at Hitchin, beginning next October.' On 18th May she went to Hitchin for the day. She was staying in Wimbledon, and travelled by the 12 o'clock Great Northern Express, which detached carriages at Hitchin. Rachel Cook met her on the platform and they walked up through the grounds to the house.

During the week of 22nd June she went every day to the examination hall of London University in Burlington Gardens to take the entrance exams, travelling by what she called the 'Daily bread' train at 8.30am. There were papers on arithmetic, English history and the New Testament (which she found 'delightful'). Constance took the geometry paper whilst others did French. One option was drawing, and the paper was set by the Royal Academy of Art.

On Thursday she took English Grammar and on Friday Greek, which she regretted and wished she'd opted for German. After this week of intense exam-taking following on from the weeks of study, she felt an enormous sense of anti-climax but on 28th June the news came that she had passed, 'Not with great honors *(sic)* being only 5th out of 9, but still safely in.'

On 9th October 1872 she travelled by the 5 o'clock 'express for Cambridge with the slip-carriage for Hitchin.' *(See Appendix 2.)*

Constance Maynard was the first Girtonian to take the Moral Science Tripos, gaining a Class II in 1876.

Eliza Baker, (1854-1924) was born on 25th July 1854, in Bridgewater, Somerset, the daughter of Thomas Baker, a draper, and his wife Ann Tiver. She was educated at North London Collegiate School, of which the Head was Miss Buss, before going to the College. She gained a College Certificate of Proficiency in Political Economy, Class III in 1876 and a Class I in the History Special Exam in June 1877.

Constance Mary Shorrock, (d.1905) attended the College and at some point married and became Mrs Malim but nothing else is known about her.

Standing: (left to right) Isabella Gamble, Rachel Cook,
Professor E C Clark, Louisa Lumsden, Amy Bulley.
Seated: Sarah Woodhead, Emily Gibson and Isabella Townshend
Benslow House, c. 1871

Chapter 3

The Lectures and the Lecturers

From the beginning Emily Davies was adamant that there should be no concessions to the women at the College and that they should follow the same course of study as the men at Cambridge. In her memoir Anna Lloyd notes that, 'Miss Davies was determined that the College should be a real College and not a new variety of girls' school.'

One problem with this was that the women had not received the same education as the men up to the point when they entered the College. It was very rare for a girl to be taught Greek or Latin, and mathematics was usually limited to simple arithmetic.

Consequently the applicants had to spend a great deal of time before they went up to the College learning the basics of these subjects. Jane Dove, who entered the College in 1871, noted in her memoir that they had 'absolutely no knowledge of the elementary classics and mathematics, which absorbed most of our time to begin with.' She also says: 'the great event of our days, of course, was the arrival of lecturers who came by train either from London or Cambridge, usually about two o'clock'.

One of the prime reasons for choosing Hitchin as the location for the College was that it was roughly equidistant between London and Cambridge. Benslow House was conveniently close to the railway station. This meant that lecturers from both London and Cambridge Universities would be able to visit, though the journey took rather longer in the late 1860s than it does today.

In her address given at Girton College during the Old Student's Session, August 1907, Louisa Lumsden remembered that there were just four lecturers in the first term of the College in 1869. They were John Seeley, E.C. Clark, James Stuart and Fenton Hort. Mr Seeley came from London, Mr Clark and Mr Stuart from Cambridge, and Fenton Hort was the rector of the nearby parish of St Ippolyts. Anna Lloyd wrote to her friend, Mary Pease, in November 1870 telling her:

> *We have for Greek Mr Clark, three times a week; for Latin Mr Graves and Mr Stanwell each once a week (they are really the same man divided into two for convenience), Mr Brown for Divinity once a week, Dr Althous, German once a week. With all the capital teaching we get, I am sorry so few English women can and do, avail themselves of the privilege.*

In her memoir 'Reminiscences of Hitchin College', published in the *Girton Review* in May 1925, Emily Gibson wrote:

> *Our teaching during the first term was scanty but excellent. Mr E.C. Clark came twice a week from Cambridge for both Latin and Greek. We took the set subjects for the year's Little-go, a book of Herodotus and a Latin Play and went through them very slowly. It was very elementary work, for we were all beginners, but the class*

was small and eager and Mr. Clark the most patient, painstaking and thorough of teachers, so that we got on pretty quickly and enjoyed the lectures immensely.

John Robert Seeley had published, at first anonymously, *Ecce Homo: a Survey of the Life and Work of Jesus Christ.* This was a controversial document in which Seeley concluded that a reconsideration of 'the speculative commonwealth of Christ' would 'add a new chapter to the science of politics'. He may have wished it to be anonymous but by 1869 when he travelled from London to Hitchin it seems the students knew who the author was and Emily Gibson went on to say:

For a single term we had lectures on English from Mr. Seeley. This had been looked forward to as a signal honour and great opportunity, for Ecce Homo was to many of us the book of the day, but the lectures were disappointing. Seeley was not a born teacher; dry, critical and sarcastic, he demanded bricks without straw.

Fortunately her memories of Dr. Hort were quite different:

Dr. Hort, rector of St. Ippolyt's, three miles from Hitchin, who was a great authority on wild flowers and was known at Cambridge as "Hortus siccus", came once a week to lecture on Paley's Evidences; a dull subject, but we liked the lecturer and used often to walk over to his charming little country church to hear him preach on Sunday. He was a shy quiet man with a troublesome stammer, but one thought of him as a student and something of a saint.

Fenton John Anthony Hort (1828-1892) was a complex character who has been described by Graham Patrick in the *Oxford Dictionary of Biography* as 'one of the last Renaissance men, before knowledge became fragmented into specialisms'.

Hort's personal interest was botany but at Trinity College, Cambridge he studied classics and mathematics, gaining a first class award in the Classical Tripos in 1850 and a year later first class awards in both the Moral Science Tripos and the Natural Science Tripos.

He was a fellow of Trinity College and was active in the foundation of the Working Men's College in Cambridge. He was ordained into the Church of England as a deacon in 1854 and as priest at Ely Cathedral in 1856. In 1857 he married Fanny Holland with whom he had five sons, one of whom died in infancy.

Marriage meant he had to give up the fellowship and Trinity College presented him with the living of St Ippolyts-cum-Great Wymondley near Hitchin. He continued to work on theological texts and translations but missed the life of the academic in Cambridge.

The opportunity to lecture to the students at the College seems to have been very welcome. He was able to return to Cambridge in 1887 when he was elected to the Lady Margaret professorship of divinity. Louisa Lumsden remembered that Dr. Hort 'selected the Acts of the Apostles for his theme, St Luke being the actual book required for the Little-go. Nevertheless all the students passed the Little- go.'

James Stuart (1843-1913) taught mathematics in the first term the college opened. He gave the first ever lecture in the College. Louisa Lumsden was expecting a 'dignified elderly person, perhaps with a long white beard' and was quite amazed when the youthful figure of James Stuart jauntily entered the room.

She was even more amazed to hear his Scottish accent revealing his place of origin as Fife, close to her own home. In her address at Girton in 1907 she goes on to say:

> *Moreover, he there and then plunged us into Conic Sections! It was intensely interesting, that I must admit, but it was also highly bewildering.*

Despite their unfamiliarity with mathematics the students enjoyed their lectures from James Stuart and liked him very much. Unfortunately he contracted measles at the end of the first term and was replaced by **Fletcher Moulton** (1844-1921) who was a brilliant mathematician and fellow of Christ's College, Cambridge. In her 1925 *Reminiscences* Emily Gibson recalled:

> *His keenness was catching. He was a tall lank creature, rather out of scale with the blackboard, and I have seen him fling himself on his knees before it in his eagerness to make some point clear to our dull brains.*
>
> *Sarah Woodhead and I were alone in his class, for we were the only students, of the first five, reading for the Mathematical Tripos. And I am afraid we both found him dangerously fascinating.*

Fascinating as Fletcher Moulton might have been, Emily Gibson's allegiance wavered. She had begun to take an interest in political economy and in her third year attended the lectures given by **John Venn** (1834-1923).

Influenced by John Stuart Mill, Venn lectured in moral sciences. In 1866 he had published The Logic of Chance and developed the theory of probability, eventually designing the Venn diagram, a series of overlapping circles to illustrate relationships. At the end of their course with Venn the students were examined by John Stuart Mill.

A name that occurs several times during the years of planning before the College opened is **Sedley Taylor.** He was a great enthusiast for women's education but because he had not been ordained it was difficult for him to hold a fellowship at Cambridge.

He had been bursar at Trinity College until 1869 and when this post ceased he continued to reside in Trinity until his death without a post in the college, though he was librarian of Trinity in 1870-71. He was fortunate in having a private income, which enabled him to follow his love of music, and he became a noted philanthropist in Cambridge.

He was very much in favour of the College being located in Cambridge decrying the fact that too much of lecturers' time was taken up with travelling to Hitchin and commenting on the expense of the train journey. He also recognised that in Hitchin the students were far removed from the libraries and museums that the undergraduates of the other colleges were able to use.

Sedley Taylor was right to be concerned about the isolation of the students. The lecturers each visited once or twice a week and the length of the lecture depended as much on the times of the trains as on the subject being taught. In between the lectures the students had very little support in their studies, though Emily Davies mentions

Julia Wedgwood being a help in this respect. (There are several references to Julia Wedgwood. She seems to have been a great supporter of the College and spent some time there, though she never registered as a student).

Some of the students found the effort and determination needed too much and left the College before completing the course. For others it was the demands of family that forced their withdrawal from the College. Those that did persevere travelled to Cambridge to take the examinations. Frances Dove reported that

> *'Towards the end of 1872 came the great event of the Classical Tripos, and Miss Cook and Miss Lumsden went off with Miss Davies to Cambridge. They stayed at the University Arms and I believe their papers were brought to them there and written under Miss Davies' superintendence.'*

In fact the event was not quite as smooth as this report might indicate. The two women sat with Miss Davies in the University Arms Hotel waiting for the papers to be delivered. In her address to the Girton College Old Students' Session in 1907 Louisa Lumsden:

> *...remembered the first morning at the University Arms. We settled in our sitting-room, pen in hand, expectant of the paper, while Miss Davies knitted away steadily by the fire – I can hear the click of her needles still! But minute after minute slipped away and still, until a whole hour had gone by, no paper came...When at last the messenger came, he had, it appeared, been sent to a wrong address. My nerves were all in a quiver and work was almost impossible. Miss Cook took it with superior calm.*

Louisa Lumsden was sure that this unfortunate incident was the cause of her poor result, a Third Class, whilst Rachel Cook took a Second Class.

Sarah Woodhead had taken, and passed, the Mathematical Tripos earlier, so she, Rachel Cook and Louisa Lumsden were the first women ever to take the Cambridge University examinations, truly the Girton Pioneers. When the news reached Benslow House there was great rejoicing.

Back row: left to right Rachel Cook, Louisa Lumsden, Elizabeth Welsh, Amy Bulley, Sarah Woodhead, Mary Hoskins
Middle row: Mary Kingsland, Rose Aitken, Jane Dove
Front row: Emily Gibson, Isabella Townshend, Isabella Gamble
Benslow House, c. 1871/2

Chapter 4

Life at the College

On October 16th 1869 Benslow House was ready to receive the first students. Isabella Townshend and Sarah Woodhead had won the scholarships and for the others the fee was £35 for an eight-week term. Emily Gibson wrote at a later date:

> *The door was opened, and on the threshold there stood the keen little lady to whose courage and energy the whole scheme for a College for women was due, and who was now quivering with excitement, thinly veiled in a business-like manner, in this moment when her hopes were actually beginning to materialise.*

All the women were very excited about their new and rather daring venture. Just before going to Hitchin **Anna Lloyd** wrote:

> *The house is so small that we cannot have two rooms each – we shall have to sleep in our study or study in our sleeping room – whichever sounds best. I saw the ground plan of Benslow House, Hitchin, and have chosen a bedroom*

*19ft by 13ft. It has a large cupboard – which
I purpose to hide my bath and washing affairs*

In her later memoir she recalled an incident in the train
as she was travelling towards London.

*I was scarcely seated in the train, when a
clergyman in the railway carriage said to two
ladies, 'Ha! This is Hitchin, and that, I believe
is that infidel place.' I remember the fire that
flushed my face as I said, 'Oh no, not infidel,
why do you say that?' and how I then explained
that the College for Women was founded on
the same principles as the men's colleges of
Cambridge and did not their founders desire
and provide religious observance? I can recall
the recoil with which the ladies eyed me, but
the clergyman shook hands as he left the train,
and said he was glad I could give such a good
account of affairs.*

In a letter to Mary H. Pease in March 1870 she gave a
detailed description of a typical timetable for a day. They
were woken at 7.15am and prayers were held in the library
at 8 o'clock, followed by breakfast.

The morning was free for study and 'from 12 until 3
lunch and walking goes on … some study until nearly
2pm, others lunch soon after 12', which indicates a fair
amount of informality in the lunch arrangements which
differs from the account of the dining room being arranged
with a 'high' table for the staff with the students sitting
in a line at a table before it, an arrangement that they
objected to because it made conversation difficult.

Lectures took place between 3 o'clock and 5.30pm and
were somewhat constrained by the times of the trains
to and from Hitchin. Dinner was at 6 o'clock and the

evenings were taken up with more study and a variety of activities that the students devised as time went on. Prayers at 8 o'clock in the morning were not compulsory. On her second day at the College Constance Maynard was too late for prayers because she 'waited for Miss Woodhead to go (which she never does being a Quaker)'.

A group was formed known as 'The College Five'. A record was kept of the meetings and the first members were Dorothy *(sic)* Gibson, Anna Lloyd, Louisa Lumsden, Isabel Townshend, Sarah Woodhead and Rachel Cook. (For the first term there were only five students, Rachel Cook joining them after Christmas in 1870.)

The reference to 'Dorothy Gibson' is something of a mystery – Miss Gibson was Emily Caroline, not Dorothy. It seems the students referred to each other as Miss and it is possible that they were unsure of each other's first name.

The honorary members were Emily Davies, Elizabeth Adelaide Manning, Julia Wedgwood and Emily Sherreff. Elizabeth Manning had taken the entrance exam and been admitted but did not want to take any further exams. She was the stepdaughter of Charlotte Manning, the mistress of the College in 1869.

Julia Wedgwood was a supporter of the College and spent some time there, but was not a student. Emily Sherreff succeeded Charlotte Manning as Mistress. The first meeting of 'The College Five' was on 26th October 1869 at which the members each read a poem.

These included 'Abt Vogler' by Browning, 'To a Skylark' by Shelley and 'Fidelity' by Wordsworth. It is not recorded whether or not these poems were also discussed but by 12th March 1870 the group seems to have developed into more of a debating society with subjects such as 'Is there no other way of arriving at the Truth than by reason?'

'What is the best incentive to acquirement of knowledge?' and 'Being a man, what career would you choose?'

Constance Maynard, who was at the College from 1872, remembered that 'Sunday evening was spent by the first students, known by then as the Pioneers, and their friends in reading up the politics of the week, and in general discussion.'

Sunday was also, of course, the day they went to church, or in the case of several of the students, to Quaker Meeting. Hitchin had a large Quaker community at this time and Constance mentioned in her diary how much she enjoyed visiting one of Hitchin's prominent Quakers, Lawson Thompson, and his wife for tea on 7th December 1872 when she saw Samuel Lucas' sketches and Lawson Thompson's Quaker portraits.

Music was an important part of the recreational activities. There was a piano in the house and it is likely that most of the students would have been able to play a little. Amy Bulley was an accomplished pianist and accompanied the others when they sang part-songs.

The students also attended a weekly singing class run by Mr Gainsford, vicar of St Saviour's Church nearby, and they would walk back up Benslow Lane singing the songs they had learnt and others that they had composed.

Physical exercise was very important to the women at Benslow House and most of them tried to have some exercise every day. An open-air swimming pool in Queen Street had opened in 1860. From April until November it was open from 5.30am until 9.00pm, and sessions cost 3d each.

There were ladies' sessions on three mornings and one evening a week. Constance Maynard found it a 'fine open place & very clear water, but tremendously cold.' Cold it may have been but the women at the College seem to have made good use of this facility though some were evidently better swimmers than others; Miss Gibson once rescued Miss Lumsden from drowning!

Jane Dove was a stronger swimmer and she 'once swam up and down it, having carefully measured it and made allowances for turning, until I had swum a mile.' Again Constance Maynard's diary tells us that in May 1873 she went 'to the baths with Lumsden, Dove and Bulley ...all were amused by my diving & then quite slowly floating to the top – as my face emerged I heard "O Maynard, you look so pretty – exactly as if you were dead!".' And all this in voluminous 19th century bathing dresses!

Miss Lumsden, however, excelled in other areas. She was known as being able to 'do the trapeze' and was good at games. It could not have been easy to play games on the sloping grounds of Benslow House but Mr Tomkinson, who was a great supporter of Miss Davies and her enterprise and had been instrumental in establishing the College, taught them to play fives, and they tried to play football, but this was going too far for Miss Davies and she forbade it. However, on 19th March 1873 Constance Maynard recorded that they did play football in the garden. In the summer 'cricket was all the rage' with Lumsden and Maynard as captains.

Both Louisa Lumsden and Constance Maynard remembered one incident when Miss Davies did 'let down her hair'. One day Miss Maynard was rolling the lawn with the heavy iron roller when some of the other women decided to 'walk' on the roller as it was pulled along. Miss Davies saw this and said, 'I believe I could do that. Will you hold my hand?' At which, holding lightly on to Constance Maynard's hand, she 'walked' from one end of the lawn to the other. In her memoirs Constance Maynard remarked,

'Her life seemed so much apart from us, so solitary, that a "human" incident like this was refreshing.'

Gymnastics was part of the college curriculum and there was a fair amount of provision made with a hand swing and rope ladders in the loft. Athletics were taken outside but when it was wet were held in the library, 'leaping and wrestling', according to Constance Maynard. 'Bathing costumes and long hair gave a very amusing effect.' A few days later her gymnastics dress arrived but, unfortunately, she does not describe it.

In a letter to Barbara Bodichon Jane Dove remembered nightingales singing in the grounds and that they took the 'train to Stevenage and walked to the woods at Knebworth' where they found 'yellow nettle and other treasures'.

Walking back they 'had the road to ourselves. We marched along singing college songs. I'm afraid Miss Davies would have been sadly horrified.' Other walks they took were to the surrounding villages, such as St Ippolyts, Gosmore and Charlton, enjoying the open countryside that separated them from Hitchin at that time.

In her memoir of 1907 Louisa Lumsden remembers walking to Wain Wood and to Lilley and the Dykes and finding a flower called Dane's blood, which she thought was an orchid. It is, in fact, *Campanula glomerata,* or Clustered Bellflower, which grows on the chalk of the Chilterns. Less energetic pastimes included walking up the hill after dinner to 'walk on the edge of the cliff and see the Edinburgh express slip its carriage.'

One activity that caused a furore was when the students decided to perform scenes from Swinburne's *Atalanta in Calydon* and from *Much Ado About Nothing* and *Twelfth Night* by Shakespeare. Rachel Cook was Benedict and Louisa Lumsden was Malvolio and both performed in men's clothes.

Even though these performances were given in the privacy of the library Miss Davies strongly objected to the students wearing men's clothes.

Barbara Bodichon visited the College to speak with Emily Gibson, who was deemed to be the 'ring-leader' to reason with her. Miss Gibson had, however, just gone into mourning and as a protest against the fussy fashions of the time, had designed and made a dress for herself based on the new 'rational dress'.

It had no waistband and fell in plain folds at the back from the neck to the heel with a little smocking or gathering at the front. Though Madame Bodichon had gone to reprimand she was enchanted by the dress and asked for the pattern so she could have one made for herself.

In January 1872 Sarah Woodhead had done very well in the Mathematics Tripos and by March 1873 Rachel Cook and Louisa Lumsden were ready to sit the Classical Tripos. Accompanied by Emily Davies, they went to Cambridge and stayed at the University Arms where they sat for the exam while Miss Davies knitted.

Despite the mix-up in the delivery of the papers which caused some anxiety, they both passed; Miss Lumsden with a third class and Miss Cook with a second. Constance Maynard recorded in her diary on 22nd March, 'I went with Bulley and Gamble [and] borrowed two flags from the Independent Chapel School, carrying them through the town.

Waylaid Mr Moulton – no further news – so celebrations – bell-ringing demonstrations – had to be postponed.' Within days they had 'News at last from Cambridge! ... we put two flags on stilts by the chimney, sat in a pie on the roof singing "The Pioneers", rang the great fire-bell and dinner-bell and promiscuously rushed everywhere for an hour.' In later life others remembered that the ringing of the bells brought out the Hitchin fire brigade.

Their jubilation was well justified. The examiners told Emily Davies that 'Rachel Cook's translation of Aristotle was the best in the whole examination and the two examiners who looked over it are in raptures' and Louisa Lumsden's paper on Roman history was 'one of the prettiest shown up'.

Earlier Sarah Woodhead had achieved 'Senior Optima' in the Mathematics Tripos, which year were the hardest papers ever known. (Sadly, none was allowed to proceed beyond the level of the ordinary BA degree and they were not eligible, as women, to have the degree conferred upon them, receiving only a degree certificate. At the conferring of the mathematical degree on the men, however, the male students cried, 'and now three cheers for the lady!')

Apart from the scandal of the acting episode there were other things that the students found less than satisfactory at the College; they found it irksome that they had to ask permission to be away from Benslow House, they complained that the food was too plain and insufficient, the beds were too narrow, the sheets too short and the mirrors too small and too high. Louisa Lumsden complained that on February 20th 1870 the thermometer registered 35 degrees Fahrenheit all day and the chimneys smoked.

It had never been intended that Benslow House should be a permanent location for the College and by 1873 it was becoming quite crowded, even with the corrugated iron 'tabernacle' in the garden to provide extra accommodation. In the years since 1869 plans for a purpose-built College nearer Cambridge had been afoot.

Land had been purchased in the village of Girton at a cost of £1924 11s 3d, and buildings designed by Alfred Waterhouse in the fashionable neo-Gothic style. The students had been extremely resourceful in the four years they were in Hitchin but the fact remained that they were isolated from the libraries and social life of the University and those students who were to transfer looked forward to widening their horizons three miles, rather than thirty, from the centre of Cambridge.

Frances Dove was the first student to set foot in the new building. Constance Maynard's diary entry for October 17th 1873 records that there was a lot of noise and there were 'thirty-five workmen in the house and they will not be out till Xmas.'

Clustered Bellflower

Eliza Baker, Constance Maynard
and Constance Shorrock (seated)

Chapter 5

What they did next

As might be expected of a group of women who showed such determination to get to the College in the first place, many of them went on to further the cause of women in society, making huge differences in many areas but especially education and women's franchise. Those who worked actively for this cause tended to be members, or at least sympathisers, with the suffragist movement, rather than the militant suffragettes. Some left the College and disappeared from the record, but a significant number of these Pioneering Women left an interesting legacy.

Louisa Lumsden was 28 when she first made the journey to Benslow House in Hitchin to be one of the first five students or "Pioneers", who formed the College in 1869. Emily Davies noted that she is 'manifestly a lady, as well as an eager student, and I should think

eminently desirable for us to have in our first group'. Louisa was disappointed to achieve only a third class pass in the Classical Tripos in 1873, which she later put down to nervousness and the tension of not knowing whether the women would be able to sit the exam at all until the hour it was appointed to begin.

Even with this low pass Louisa was invited to be the classical tutor at the new college site at Girton, but it was not only Miss Davies' knitting whilst they waited for the exam papers to be delivered that she found difficult to accommodate: the two women were less than compatible and Louisa resigned in 1875.

In 1876 she was appointed classics mistress at Cheltenham Ladies' College, accompanied by Constance Maynard. The following year they were both recruited to head a new school for girls in St Andrews, Fife, with Louisa as headmistress and Constance as head teacher. The school had high academic aspirations with a house system and a sixth form. Another alumna of the College, Jane Frances Dove, taught science at the school.

Once a project had been started and had become well established it seems Louisa's commitment to it waned. Her relationship with Constance Maynard was in difficulties and Constance left St Andrews in 1880, to become the first mistress of Westfield College, London University's first women's residential college, in Hampstead in 1882.

Louisa's mother's ill health led her to resign as headmistress in 1882 and she returned to the Highlands to be with her. After her mother's death in late 1883, and visiting Canada and the United States in the summer of 1884, she applied for the post of mistress of Girton.

She missed election by one vote but was not entirely sorry about this. She recorded in her autobiography,

Yellow Leaves, 'I have suffered so much at Girton'. She stayed in Glenbogie, living alone except for a dog that friends had given her, spending her time serving on school boards until 1895 when she was asked to return to St Andrews as warden of a new hall of residence for women at the university.

This project was also beset with difficulties with a lot of opposition from the university. The system of living in hall was not a part of the Scottish tradition but she persevered for five years, winning the respect of both residents and some non-residents. She was frequently in conflict with the committee concerning the extent of her powers as warden until in 1900, depressed and ill, she resigned as warden.

The next few years were spent with her sister, Rachel, travelling in Scotland and on the continent until Rachel died in 1908, when Louisa moved to Aberdeen.

By now Louisa was 68 but new interests and work were opening up to her. She believed passionately in the cause for women's suffrage, working for the non-militant suffragists, and became president of the Aberdeen Suffrage Association and one of ten vice-presidents of the Scottish Churches' League for Woman Suffrage.

In an essay on the position of women in history in 1911 she blamed the Protestant Reformation as the root of women's servile status. In 1917 she was instrumental in setting up the Scottish Women's Rural Institutes, the aim of which was to broaden women's horizons.

An honorary LLD (Doctor of Laws) degree was conferred upon her by St Andrews in 1911 (Cambridge still didn't confer degrees on women) and during the First World War she used her powers of oratory on behalf of the war effort.

She spoke at the Girton jubilee in 1919, and in 1925 was created Dame of the British Empire in recognition of her services to education.

Louisa Lumsden died on 2nd January 1935 at the age of ninety-four.

Rachel Cook. One of the first six students at the College, Rachel Cook was the first woman to attempt the Classical Tripos at Cambridge, gaining a second class in 1873.

On graduating (but without a degree being conferred upon her because women were not eligible for Cambridge degrees until 1949), she served on the governing body of Girton College for several years.

In the year after leaving Girton Rachel married Charles Prestwich Scott, who was the editor of the *Manchester Guardian,* and subsequently had four children. Rachel lived in Manchester for the rest of her life.

Rachel's enthusiasm for women's education remained as strong as ever, and between 1877 and 1883 she was instrumental in setting up the Manchester and Salford College for Women, being the driving force in the campaign and acting as secretary to the college. In 1883 women were not only admitted to Manchester's Victoria University but were also eligible for degrees. In this work she was supported by her husband and the *Manchester Guardian.*

Apart from work for women's higher education, Rachel also worked for the improvement of education for women and girls at all levels. She was a member of the committee of Manchester High School for Girls, was one of the founders of Withington Girls' School and had an interest in the progressive co-educational school, Ladybarn House, Cheadle. In her work as a member of Manchester's school board she advocated free education for elementary school children.

Rachel was also active politically. As might be expected she was an ardent supporter of women's suffrage and also spoke eloquently on other social issues.

Rachel continued to exercise her literary skills throughout her life, contributing copy to the *Manchester Guardian* and translating Tacitus' *Agricola* in 1885 and Honoré de Balzac's *Une fille d'Eve* and *Mémoires de jeunes mariées.*

She died at her home in Fallowfield, Manchester on November 27th 1905 at the early age of fifty-seven.

Frances Dove was 24 when her father told her about the College. Having prepared for the entrance examination herself she was placed sixth of the eleven candidates.

After two years in Hitchin she had the distinction of being the first student to set foot in the new college building at Girton in 1873. She and Mary Kingsland were the first women to take the Natural Science Tripos in 1873. This success admitted them to the university lectures in anatomy, physiology and chemistry.

Miss Beale, head of Cheltenham Ladies' College, engaged Frances to teach mathematics and physiology, and she was followed there by Louisa Lumsden and Constance Maynard. When Louisa Lumsden was appointed headmistress of St Andrews School for Girls in Fife, both Frances Dove and Constance Maynard joined her on the staff.

Living and working in the same establishment proved difficult for three such feisty women and, when Louisa Lumsden resigned, Frances Dove became head in her place. She oversaw the move to new buildings and a change of name of the school to 'St Leonards'. Under her leadership a tradition of excellence was established and by the time she resigned in 1895 the school had doubled in size.

Her reason for resigning was to establish a school for girls in England along the lines of the existing Public Schools for boys. As a result Wycombe Abbey School opened in September 1896 in a house near High Wycombe purchased from Lord Carrington. Opening with just forty pupils the school had grown to 230 pupils and fifty mistresses by the time Frances Dove retired in 1910.

She may have retired as headmistress but for the next few years Frances Dove pursued her interest in local politics. In 1907 she stood for High Wycombe town council and in 1908 was nominated for mayor. At this time, though she was a supporter of the non-militant suffragists, the militant actions of the suffragettes turned public opinion against her and she was prevented from becoming the first woman mayor in England. In 1921 she was made a JP for Buckinghamshire and though well into her 70s learned to drive in order to fulfil her duties.

Apart from these political and social activities she was a member of Girton College council from 1902 to 1924, after which she became a life governor. She was awarded a DBE in January 1928.

Frances Dove never married and died at her home in High Wycombe on 21ˢᵗ June 1942 at the age of ninety-four.

Elizabeth Welsh attended the College from September 1872 and on completing her course of study was offered a Girton College classical lectureship in 1875.She felt unable to accept this post, as there was some question about the previous holder's position. Instead she took a teaching post at Manchester High School at the very acceptable salary of £200 per annum.

The following year she did return to Girton as a lecturer and demanded an equivalent salary. She was an excellent teacher and none of her students failed the 'Little-go' examination. This was a great achievement given that very few girls had studied Latin before going to Cambridge.

As Girton College grew and a Vice-Mistress was needed, Elizabeth was appointed to the post in 1883 and also became garden steward in the same year. Much of the landscaping of the college grounds was her work. She became Mistress of the college in 1885 and oversaw the third building programme, which included a chapel and extended the student accommodation from 70 to 120 places.

Elizabeth Welsh took her pastoral duties as Mistress very seriously. She was known as an approachable and kindly adviser, and testimonials she wrote for students demonstrate her shrewd judgement. Unfortunately she did not enjoy good health, suffering from neuralgia which prevented her from taking a very active part in the social life of the college.

As with several of the other women who attended the College she took an interest in social concerns. She helped to set up a subscription fund to provide a nurse to work in the village of Girton where there were at that time many impoverished farm labourers and their families.

On retirement Elizabeth returned to Londonderry and then moved to Lyme Regis before moving, three years before her death, to Edinburgh where she became the focal point for former students in the area. She never married and died at her home in Morningside, Edinburgh on 13th February 1921 aged seventy-eight. She was buried in Girton village churchyard.

Mary Ann Kingsland won an exhibition to the College for Women in Hitchin in 1871, and she and Jane Frances Dove were the first women to take the Natural Science Tripos. Mary Kingsland gained a second-class honours in 1873 though, of course, no degree was conferred.

She moved with the College to Girton and after she finished her studies became an assistant lecturer there for eighteen months. She went on to teach at the grammar school for girls in Bradford and later at the Saltaire School, Shipley. Marriage in 1879 to a Congregational minister, the Rev. Thomas Kilpin Higgs (1851-1907), resulted in her work for the church, and four children. After several moves the family eventually settled in Oldham in 1890 where Thomas was minister of Greenacres Congregational Church until his death in 1907.

Under her married name of Mary Higgs, Mary Kingsland wrote and lectured on a wide variety of social issues such as child development and unemployment, setting up summer schools for the study of social questions and advocating family allowances and widowed mothers' pensions. Her home became the base for many welfare organizations.

Puzzled as to why women in need were avoiding the 'safe-house' and women's lodging houses she had set up, she disguised herself as a tramp and experienced the conditions the poor lived in for herself, which she wrote up in *Glimpses into the Abyss (1906)*. She became an acknowledged authority on the destitute, and gave evidence at inquiries and played an important part in the founding of the National Association for Women's Lodging Houses in 1909.

During the First World War her opposition to conscription led her to join the Religious Society of Friends and through the Quakers she continued her work with the Vagrancy Reform Society. She worked tirelessly until her death at her daughter's house in Greenwich in 1937. One of her last achievements was to edit *The Way to the Joyous Life,* a selection of W. T. Stead's devotional writings, illustrating the spiritual side of her nature.

Just before her death in 1937 at the age of eighty-three, Mary Higgs was awarded an OBE for her services to Oldham.

 **Agnes Amy Bulley** became a student at the College in 1871. She moved to Girton with the College in 1873 but then wanted to extend her studies by a year, which was denied her by Girton. As a result she moved to the more recently opened Newnham College and completed her studies there. She was one of the first women to sit the Moral Science Tripos and was placed in the second class.

From 1876 until 1885 Amy Bulley was an assistant mistress at Manchester High School for Girls and during this time she became involved with a newly formed movement for the advancement of academic education for girls and women.

This resulted in the setting up of the Manchester and Salford College for Women in 1877 with Amy Bulley as its secretary, a post she held until 1883 when the college was replaced by a women's department as part of Owen's College.

After leaving Manchester High School she became interested in women's employment and the labour movement. She began to contribute to the *Manchester Guardian* and write articles for other journals on political issues, and became a distinguished journalist. She supported women's suffrage but with caution.

The Manchester, Salford and District Women's Trades Union Council was founded in 1895 and Amy Bulley served as chair of the council from 1897 to 1906.

Amy Bulley was fifty-five years old in 1907 when she married Joseph Brooke (1836-1912). He was a cotton merchant and the widower of Amy's sister Mary. At this point she withdrew from public work but following his death in 1912 she moved to Bushey in Hertfordshire and once more became active in the labour movement. After the Sex Disqualification Removal Act of 1919 she became one of the first women JPs and sat on the Watford bench from 1920 to 1937.

Music was also important to Amy and she served on the council of the Watford School of Music and over the years she wrote several songs.

On 16th November 1939, at the age of eighty-seven, Amy Bulley died at her home in Bushey, Hertfordshire, of a cerebral thrombosis.

Constance Maynard. Whilst visiting cousins in St Andrews when she was twenty-three, Constance Maynard heard about a college for women that had been established in Hitchin by Emily Davies. Until then she had been resigned, though reluctantly, to marry and lead the quiet life expected of a woman of her class.

The idea that she could enrol as a student became 'an overwhelming desire'. She overcame her mother's fears that the college might be worldly and filled with people 'not at all our sort' and her father's insistence that paid employment must not be the outcome, and joined the College at Hitchin in the autumn of 1872.

She was to be in Hitchin for only a year before the College moved to Girton in 1873. She was the first Girton woman to sit for the Moral Science Tripos, gaining the equivalent of a second-class honours degree in 1875.

Her intellectual powers had been fully awakened and on

leaving Girton she joined the staff of Cheltenham Ladies' College, which her father had to allow as his business affairs were in difficulties at the time. Two years later she left with her colleague and fellow Girtonian, Louisa Lumsden, to found St Leonards School in St Andrews.

After three years Louisa and Constance's personal relationship was deteriorating. Constance was a fervent, somewhat proselytising Christian whilst Louisa's religious faith was calmer and more cerebral.

Constance was also doubting that her vocation lay in school teaching and she left to live in London, where she briefly enrolled as a student at The Slade School of Art. Before leaving Scotland she had turned down an offer of marriage from a minister. She told her sister she was unwilling to take an 'irretrievable step into bondage'.

Since 1878 London University degrees had been open to women on equal terms with men and Constance began to think about the possibility of opening a college for women based on Christian principles. At the same time a spinster of independent means, Ann Dudin Brown, was thinking of setting up a college for missionaries.

A meeting with Constance persuaded Miss Brown to put her money into the foundation of a college for women as part of London University. In October 1882 Westfield College opened in Hampstead with one lecturer, five students and with Constance Maynard as the Mistress, a post she was to hold for thirty-three years.

Each week Constance held a Bible class and a more informal 'Function' on Sunday evenings. Not surprisingly she found that the students were more interested in philosophy than religious instruction, but, to her credit, she reworked her material accordingly. She took her pastoral role as Mistress seriously and endeavoured to know all the students personally, even when the college had grown to sixty students.

By the time she retired in 1913 there were about five hundred students, which must have made it more difficult to know them all. Though they were her substitute family she clearly felt the lack of a deep personal relationship and suffered from bouts of depression and loneliness. She adopted a child, a six-year-old of Italian extraction, called Effie, who had been abandoned, but the relationship was not a success.

As the women's suffrage movement grew she supported it but never became actively involved. Constance was a representative of former students on Girton Executive Committee from 1881 to 1886 and a member of The Church Schools' Society from 1897 to 1905. Her notebooks record journeys to South Africa, the Holy Land, Canada and Europe and even a tour of the British Isles by bicycle.

Constance died aged eighty-six on 26th March 1935 at her home in Gerrards Cross. In her will she bequeathed £1,500 to Westfield College to fund an entrance scholarship.

Sarah Woodhead taught at Manchester High School from 1873-75 and was Head Mistress of Silverwell House School, Bolton, from 1879-81. She married C.G.B. Corbett and continued her school work after her marriage. She died at the age of fifty-seven in July 1908.

Emily Gibson married Isabella Townshend's brother, Chambre Corker Townshend. She left the College without taking the Tripos, lived for a while in Switzerland and Florence and spent some time as a sanitary inspector, what today would be thought of as a public health inspector.

Emily was a member of the Fabian Society and wrote several tracts for the society. She supported the women's suffrage movement and spent two weeks in Holloway Prison. Muriel Bradbrook, who was a student at Girton from 1927 to 1930, staying on to become, successively, a lecturer, Fellow and eventually Mistress, remembered her giving an address to students in about 1929.

She was 'an exquisitely pretty white haired old lady of eighty'. She gave the students 'one piece of really useful advice...If you ever have to go to prison, take a change of underclothes, so that they will know you are a lady; and say you are a vegetarian – the food is better if you do.'

Emily died at Ditchling, Sussex on 23 May 1934, aged eighty-five.

Mary Hoskins took the Previous exam and then left the College. It is thought she went to Paris in 1874 to study medicine.

Eliza Baker went back to her home in the West Country, where her family ran a drapery business, for a while after leaving Girton. Eliza was assistant mistress at Highfield School, Hendon, Middlesex, until 1883 and senior assistant mistress at Bedford High School from 1883 to 1884.

On 1st November 1884 she married John Lewis, who founded the John Lewis Partnership. They had two sons, John Spedan and Oswald who followed into the family business. She lived in Hampstead until her death in 1924 at the age of seventy. Her son, Oswald, donated money to Girton College to build the Eliza Baker Court in her memory in 1932.

Rose Aitken moved with the College from Hitchin to Girton and was then engaged by Miss Buss at North London Collegiate School for Girls at a salary of 100 guineas a year plus lodging. She subsequently taught at Redlands High School, Bristol, from 1874 to 1884, and Cavendish House, Cambridge from 1890 to 1895. She died at the age of seventy-five in January 1923.

There are many of the students at the College about whom we know nothing after they left but, given the determination of these young women to have taken up a place at the College at all, it is unlikely that they would have been content to live the rest of their lives in quiet domesticity.

Those that we do know about continued to work for girls' education and for higher education for women, supported the cause of women's franchise, and greater freedom and independence in general for women. It might be assumed that many of those who have passed into obscurity did so too.

Girton College, Cambridge 1873

Appendix 1

Entrance Examinations

Emily Davies was well aware that the women she wanted to attract to the College would not all have received an education that would support the expectations of Cambridge University and she, therefore, agreed to set entrance examinations in several subjects. This provided the women with an idea of the standard which they had to reach and several of them record that they spent considerable time in the weeks leading up to the examinations preparing for them. Below are examples of some of the questions that were set in 1871.

There were papers in:

Arithmetic	French
English Grammar	German
English Composition	Botany
English History	Experimental Physics
The New Testament	Geography
Latin	

The Entrance and Scholarship Examination for Hitchin College

June 1871

Arithmetic   2½ hours

1. Write in words 24763517.

2. Divide 8381466 by 369

3. In 8179165 inches, how many miles, and in the same number of square inches, how many acres?

4. Add together ⁴⁄₁₅, 1⅓ , 5⅕, ⁷⁄₃₈

5. Find the value in Pounds of ⅖, of ³⁄₁₁, of 2⅐, of 8871 pence.

English Composition   2 hours

1. Give a succinct account of the plot of Shakespeare's As You Like It.

2. Write an essay on the advantage or disadvantage of metre.

The following will be accepted as alternative subjects:

1. Write a brief account of the history of England during the reign of James I.

2. Give a minute description of two of three well-known pictures.

History

Four out of eight questions had to be answered. One of the eight to choose from was:

Write a short account of Wycliffe or Joan of Arc.

Geography

As in the History and English papers, there was a choice of questions, two of them being:

Sketch one of the following maps with the chief rivers and mountain ranges:

United States and Canada

British India

European Turkey and the Austro-Hungarian Empire-Kingdom.

Ireland

Mention the principal seats of volcanic action existent or extinct, on the earth, and give any particulars known to you of the range of special manifestations of this kind of action.

Appendix 2

Some railway notes

Phil Rowe

It is hard to appreciate the revolutionary effect of the coming of the railway in the mid-nineteenth century. Twenty years before the College opened its doors for the first time, there was no railway in Hitchin, and the time taken to travel to and from Cambridge and London by coach would have made the arrangements for visiting lecturers difficult in the extreme.

Although a train service from Maiden Lane through Hitchin to York had been launched in 1850 (King's Cross station did not open until October 1852) the intricacies of railway company politics prevented any through service to Cambridge until as late as 1866. The timetable established then was more or less unchanged in 1869 and is shown overleaf.

Fares were not cheap compared with the average earnings of a working man, and one can understand that the cost of lecturers travelling between Hitchin and both Cambridge and London was a significant consideration in the decision to move from Benslow to Girton.

Today we are used to a frequent, regular-interval service of trains on this line, but in 1869 there were but three fast trains between Hitchin and Cambridge, together with four slower ones, all with connections to and from London.

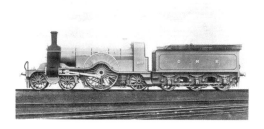

Great Northern Railway express passenger locomotive ('Stirling Single') of 1870

A feature of the train service that is mentioned more than once in the students' correspondence is the use of 'slip carriages'. The 9am, 12 noon and 5pm trains from King's Cross for York and the north did not stop at Hitchin, but one or two carriages for Cambridge were attached to the rear of these expresses. On the approach to Hitchin a 'brakesman' in the rear portion would disconnect the coupling from the rest of the train, and bring the now free-wheeling section to a gentle stand in Hitchin station while the rest of the train continued at speed on its way north. Once safely in Hitchin, the Cambridge carriages would be coupled to another engine which would take Cambridge-bound passengers for the remainder of their journey.

Hitchin station   c. 1870

HITCHIN, BALDOCK, ROYSTON, SHEPRETH, and CAMBRIDGE.—Great Northern.

Fares from London			Down.	1,2,3	1&2	1,2,3	1&2	1,2,3	1&2	1&2	SUNDAYS	1,2,3	1,2,3
1 cl.	2 cl.	3 cl.	King's Cross Sta.,	mrn	mrn	mrn	mrn	aft	aft	aft		mrn	aft
			LONDON . . . dep	7e40	9 0	1027	12 0	3e50	5 0	3 15		7 30	6 0
6 0	4 6	2 8	**Hitchin** Junc. .dep	8 38	9 50	1140	1250	5 19	5 50	9 30		9 5	7 33
7 0	5 3	3 1	**Baldock**	8 47	....	1151	....	5 29	5 59	9 39		9 16	7 44
8 0	6 0	3 5½	Ashwell	8 57	....	12 1	....	5 39	....	a		9 26	7 55
8 6	6 6	3 9½	**Royston**	9 7	1010	1211	1310	5 49	6 14	9 57		9 36	8 4
9 6	7 6	3 0½	Meldreth	9 14	....	1218	....	5 56	....	a		9 43	8 11
10 0	8 0	4 2½	**Shepreth**	9 21	....	1224	....	6 2	....	a		9 49	8 17
10 4	8 3	4 3½	Foxton	9 25	....	1228	....	6 6	....	....		9 53	8 21
10 10	8 6	4 5½	Harston	9 32	....	1233	....	6 11	c	a		9 58	8 26
11 0	8 9	4 9½	**Cambridge**	9 45	1030	1245	1330	6 23	6 35	1025		1010	8 38

Up.	1,2,3	1&2	1&2	1&2	1&2	3 cl.	1,2,3	1&2	SUNDAYS	1,2,3	1,2,3
	d	b	mrn	b	aft	aft (Wed. only.)	aft	b		mrn	aft
Cambrdg (Hill's Rd)	6 40	8 5	1010	2 2	4 0		6 30	7 20		6 55	5 30
Harston	6 53	8 17	....	2 12	....		6 42	....		7 7	5 42
Foxton	6 58	8 22	....	2 17	....		6 47	....		7 12	5 47
Shepreth	7 3	8 26	....	2 21	....		6 51	....		7 16	5 51
Meldreth	7 10	8 30	....	2 27	....		6 57	....		7 22	5 57
Royston	7 19	8 38	1035	2 35	4 20	5 5	7 5	7 41		7 30	6 5
Ashwell	7 29	8 47	....	2 45	....	5 20	7 15	....		7 40	6 15
Baldock	7 39	8 57	1049	2 54	....	5 45	7 24	7 55		7 49	6 24
Hitchin Junc. arr	7 50	9 8	1059	3 3	4 38	6 10	7 35	8 5		8 0	6 35
LONDON (K.C.) arr	9 35	1040	1150	4 0	5 35		9 3	9 20		9 35	7 45

a Stop to set down from Main Line Stations, if required. **b** 3rd class Cambridge to London. c Stops on Mondays to set down from London. **d** 3rd class from Cambridge Branch to Stations as far as Barnet, inclusive. *e* 3rd class from London.

Cambridge line timetable as published in Bradshaw's Guide for 1869

Appendix 3

Benslow House

Benslow House was built in the early part of the nineteenth century for John Ransom who owned a brick works and lime kilns.

On his death in 1867 it passed to his son, Alfred, who, having no need to live in it himself, leased it out. Henry Tomkinson acquired the lease on behalf of Emily Davies and the College for Women in 1869.

In the years since the College moved to Girton, Cambridge, the house has been used successively as a maternity home, a nursing home, and is at present a care home for the elderly.

Glossary

Double First – gaining a First Class in both parts of the Tripos

Little-go – a public examination which takes place about the middle of the course, which is less strict and important than the final one, introduced in 1824.

The Previous – another name for the Little-go.

Senior Optima – the student gaining the highest marks

Tripos, pl. triposes – The Cambridge examination system consisting of two parts. Part I is broadly based and Part II allows specialisation. Each part is awarded a Class. The Triposes covered at the College were:

> Moral Science Tripos
>
> Natural Science Tripos
>
> Classical Tripos
>
> Mathematics Tripos

Wrangler – a student who has completed the third year (called Part II) of the Mathematics Tripos with first class honours.

Sources

Bennett, Daphne – *Emily Davies and the Liberation of Women (London, 1990)*

Bradbrook, M.C. – *That Infidel Place (London, 1969)*

Forster, Margaret – *Significant Sisters: the Grassroots of Active Feminism 1839-1939 (London, 1984)*

Sondheimer, Janet – *Castle Adamant in Hampstead: A History of Westfield College (London, 1983)*

Stephen, Barbara – *Emily Davies and Girton College (London, 1927)*

Wrottesley, J.F. – *The Great Northern Railway, vol. I (London, 1979)*

The Oxford Dictionary of Biography On-line

Girton College Archives:
    The Letters of Emily Davies;
    The Letters of Barbara Bodichon;
    Other archive material

Janus: On-line Catalogue of Girton College Archives

Hitchin Museum:
    Lawson Thompson Scrapbooks;
    Other archive material

Queen Mary College, London :
    Westfield College Archives
    The Constance Maynard Archive

The National Railway Museum, York:
    Bradshaw's Railway Guide, July - December 1869

Index